Impact on Earth

The Impact of TRAVEL AND TRANSPORTATION

Nancy Dickmann

Crabtree Publishing Company

www.crabtreebooks.com

CRABTREE
PUBLISHING COMPANY
WWW.CRABTREEBOOKS.COM

Author: Nancy Dickmann

Editorial director: Kathy Middleton

Editor: Ellen Rodger

Picture Manager: Sophie Mortimer

Design Manager: Keith Davis

Children's Publisher: Anne O'Daly

Production coordinator and prepress: Ken Wright

Print coordinator: Katherine Berti

Photo credits
(t=top, b= bottom, l=left, r=right, c=center)

Front Cover: Shutterstock / T.W. van Urk, r;
All other images from Shutterstock

Interior: Alamy: Richard G. Bingham II 28, US Coast Guard
Photo 13; Science Photo Library: BeautifulChemistry.net 27;
Shutterstock: 2p2play 10, apiguide 20, Benoir Daoust 6, JJ Farq
24, Iakov Filimonov 8, Jag_cz 4, LeManna 11, 29, Olga Marc 22,
Milena Moiola 14, Monkey Business Images 23, Mopic 5, Ryan
Morgan 17, R Nagy 12, Thomas Nord 7, Alex Novikov 9, Rawpixel.
com 25, Science Photo 26, ShutterStockStudio 19, Hu Siyuan 16,
Janis Smits 15, Suwin 21, Taras Vyshnya 18.

Library and Archives Canada Cataloguing in Publication

Title: The impact of travel and transportation / Nancy Dickmann.
Names: Dickmann, Nancy, author.
Description: Series statement: Impact on Earth | Includes index.
Identifiers: Canadiana (print) 20190236779 |
  Canadiana (ebook) 20190236787 |
  ISBN 9780778774396 (hardcover) |
  ISBN 9780778774938 (paperback) |
  ISBN 9781427125187 (HTML)
Subjects: LCSH: Transportation—Environmental aspects—
  Juvenile literature. | LCSH: Travel—Environmental aspects—
  Juvenile literature.
Classification: LCC HE147.65 .D53 2020 | DDC j388—dc23

Library of Congress Cataloging-in-Publication Data

Names: Dickmann, Nancy, author.
Title: The impact of travel and transportation / Nancy Dickmann.
Description: New York , NY : Crabtree Publishing Company, 2020.
  | Series: Impact on earth | Includes index.
Identifiers: LCCN 2019053361 (print) |
  LCCN 2019053362 (ebook) |
  ISBN 9780778774396 (hardcover) |
  ISBN 9780778774938 (paperback) |
  ISBN 9781427125187 (ebook)
Subjects: LCSH: Transportation--Environmental aspects--Juvenile
  literature. | Travel--Environmental aspects--Juvenile literature.
Classification: LCC HE147.65 .D53 2020 (print) |
  LCC HE147.65 (ebook) | DDC 388--dc23
LC record available at https://lccn.loc.gov/2019053361
LC ebook record available at https://lccn.loc.gov/2019053362

Printed in the U.S.A./022020/CG20200102

Published in Canada
Crabtree Publishing
616 Welland Avenue
St. Catharines, ON
L2M 5V6

Published in the United States
Crabtree Publishing
PMB 59051
350 Fifth Ave, 59th Floor
New York, NY 10118

Contents

Getting Around

In our modern world, people are constantly on the move. We drive to work, to the store, and to see new places.

Airplanes fly overhead, carrying passengers. Trains travel beneath city streets and across the countryside. It's not just people that travel, either. Large transport trucks barrel down the highways carrying food and other goods from farms and factories to stores.

More than 100 years ago, crossing an ocean meant a long, risky journey by ship. Today, airplanes carry people safely over the ocean in a matter of hours.

Delivery Drones

Some companies are hoping to use **drones** to deliver mail-order packages. These small flying machines are powered by electricity. They bring packages directly from warehouses to homes. The goal is to deliver ordered items quickly without using delivery vans that burn fuel and create pollution.

1885 Year in which the first true automobile was built

More than 1 billion Number of cars on roads today

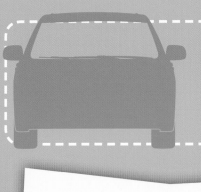

A Smaller World

More than 100 years ago, people could only travel over land on foot or by using horses or other animals. It took a long time to get anywhere, so most people never went far. Now that we have vehicles with **engines**, we can travel farther and faster.

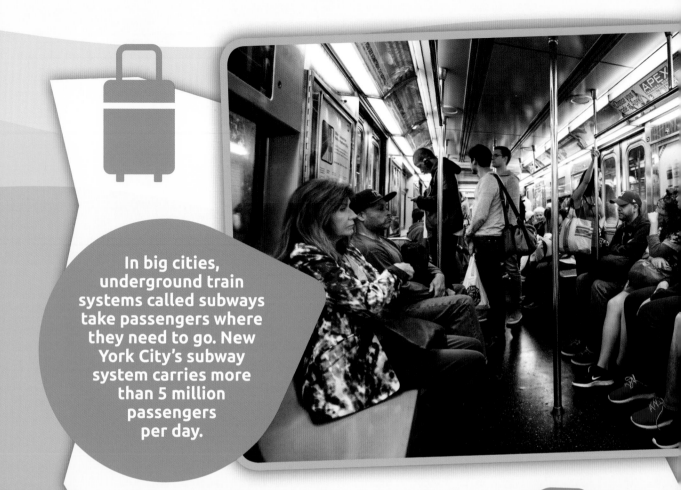

In big cities, underground train systems called subways take passengers where they need to go. New York City's subway system carries more than 5 million passengers per day.

On the Move

We depend on motor vehicles to get around. Many towns and cities are designed around cars. They have wide roads and plenty of parking. Stores are often too far for many people to walk to from their homes. In cities, people use cars, motorcycles, and buses to get where we need to go. More than 70 million new cars are built each year.

Adding Up

Airline passengers take more than 4 billion flights each year. The average American driver travels over 13,000 miles (20,900 km). Add to that millions of trucks traveling along highways delivering goods from factories to stores. Travel is a big part of our lives. It also has a big impact on the planet.

About 82% Percentage of workers commuting by car in U.S.A.

About 39% Percentage of workers who cycle to work in Antwerp, Belgium

EMERGENCY · EMERGENCY·

Disaster Averted

Transportation systems can be affected by natural disasters, sometimes with deadly results. In 2011 an earthquake struck Japan, which also triggered a **tsunami**. Many train tracks were damaged. Fortunately, Japan had put in place an automatic system that cuts power to high-speed trains when an earthquake is detected.

Why Worry?

Vehicles such as cars and trucks all need fuel to power their engines. The majority of vehicles run on fuels that come from oil.

Oil is extracted from deep underground. It is a type of **fuel** known as a **fossil fuel**. Oil can be refined, or reworked, into many different types of fuel. These fuels include gasoline, diesel, and kerosene which is used in airplanes. Burning fossil fuels creates pollution and releases gases that add to **global warming**.

Many streetcars and trains are powered by electricity. While using electricity leaves no pollution behind, fossil fuels are often burned to produce the electricity.

Plant Fuels

Not all vehicle fuels come from oil. Some cars run on ethanol, which is produced from corn or sugar cane. Ethanol is usually mixed with gasoline to make a blended fuel. Fuels that come from plants are described as **renewable** because you can grow more plants to replace the ones you use.

About 100 million Number of barrels of oil extracted each day

6,360 Number of Olympic-sized swimming pools 100 million barrels would fill

Running Out

Fossil fuels are made from the remains of living things that died long ago. Over millions of years, these remains were buried and changed by the heat and pressure underground. Once we have used up Earth's supply of fossil fuels, there will be no more. They are a non-renewable fuel.

A World of Cars

There are more people in the world than ever before, and they now have the ability to travel around the world. All that travel means more cars and trucks on the road. In crowded cities and at busy times, traffic snarls cause delays. Sitting in a traffic jam eats up valuable time and often causes stress. It also uses up more fuel than driving with no traffic.

Emergency vehicles such as ambulances sometimes get stuck in traffic jams. They can't reach the people who need them.

Driving Less

Before you make a journey by car, think about whether you could walk or cycle there instead. Riding in a vehicle that carries many passengers also reduces the impact. Is there a bus or train you could take? Could you share a ride with a friend or combine errands into a single trip?

34 hours Average number of hours per year a city commuter spends stuck in traffic in U.S.A.

Urban Sprawl

Early cities were tightly packed. People could walk where they needed to go. Today, so many people have cars that cities can grow to be huge. This is called urban sprawl. Natural areas around cities are paved over to build more roads and houses. This destroys wildlife **habitats**.

Polluting the Air

Burning fuel is a chemical reaction. It produces energy to power a vehicle, but it also creates waste products.

When a car burns fuel, the waste products come out through the exhaust pipe. Cars release gases such as **carbon dioxide**, nitrogen, and water vapor. They also produce carbon monoxide and nitrous oxides. There are also tiny pieces of soot-like matter. These are known as **particulates**. All of these waste products contribute to air pollution.

Pollution can mix with fog to form a haze called smog. But even if you can't see anything in the air, it can still be polluted.

Oil Spills

In 1989, an oil tanker called the Exxon Valdez ran aground and spilled 11 million gallons (50 million l) of oil. Oil floats, and the oil spill spread out to cover 1,300 miles (2,000 km) of the Alaskan coast. It killed hundreds of thousands of animals before it was cleaned up.

7 million **Estimated number of deaths around the world attributed by scientists to breathing polluted air**

Health Hazard

Exhaust gases go into the air, where anyone can breathe them in. Some of the gases cause serious health problems, such as heart disease, cancer, and strokes. Particulates can work their way deep into the lungs and even into the blood. They cause breathing problems.

Greenhouse Gases

The carbon dioxide (CO_2) that engines produce is an urgent problem. You cannot see or smell CO_2. This gas is found naturally in the air, and humans and animals actually breathe it out as a waste product. But the addition of hundreds of millions of vehicles over the last hundred years means CO_2 is being produced at a higher rate than ever before.

Some of the Sun's heat bounces back into space, while some gets trapped by a buildup of CO_2. This is gradually warming Earth.

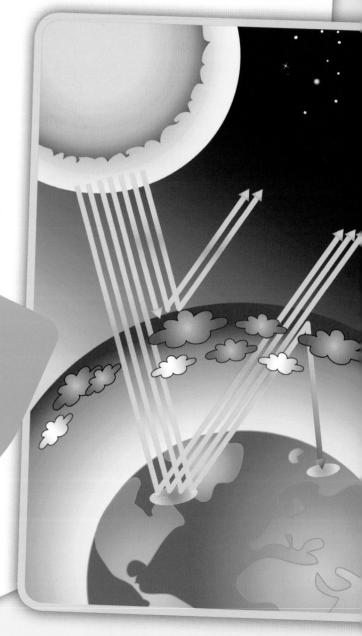

Trapping Heat

The carbon dioxide rises up into Earth's **atmosphere** and builds up, forming a sort of blanket around Earth. Normally, the Sun's rays would bounce off Earth and travel back into space, but this blanket of CO_2 is trapping rays near the planet. The gas acts like the glass in a greenhouse, keeping the heat from going back into space. This makes Earth's temperature rise, which affects climate around the world.

16.5 tons (15 metric tons)
Average amount of CO_2 released each year into atmosphere by each person in U.S.A.

WHAT CAN I DO?

Cutting Down

A lot of electricity is made by burning fossil fuels. Using less electricity means less CO_2 is released. Turn off lights and appliances when you are not using them. Only run the dishwasher or washing machine if they are full. Hang clothes outside instead of using a dryer.

Public Transportation

In some places, people have choices about how to travel. There are buses or trains to take them to work or school.

Some cities have subways or underground trains. This is called **public transportation**. Airplanes and ferries are also types of public transportation. They run on a set schedule, and anyone can ride them if they buy a ticket.

Some cities have bicycles that riders can rent by the hour. They use a smartphone app to unlock a bike.

To the Rescue!

In 2013, unusually heavy rainfall in Alberta, Canada, caused massive flooding in Calgary. The local government ordered evacuations. Tens of thousands of people had to leave their homes to escape the rising waters. The city's public transportation system stepped in to help get people out. It also helped deliver supplies to shelters.

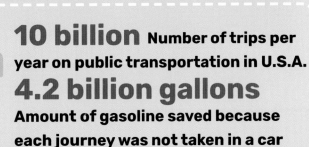

10 billion Number of trips per year on public transportation in U.S.A.

4.2 billion gallons Amount of gasoline saved because each journey was not taken in a car

Riding Together

Buses and trains use more fuel than a car, but they carry many more passengers. They use much less fuel per passenger than if everyone drove their own car. Some types of public transportation, such as underground trains, are quicker because they can't get stuck in traffic.

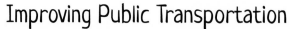

Improving Public Transportation

Public transportation helps reduce vehicle exhaust emissions, but it could be even cleaner than this. Many cities are replacing older buses with electric buses, or ones that produce very low emissions. Some buses are **hybrids**, which have a gasoline engine and an electric motor. In stop-and-go traffic, they can use the electric motor, which reduces **pollution**.

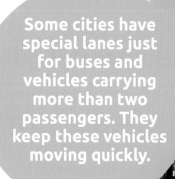

Some cities have special lanes just for buses and vehicles carrying more than two passengers. They keep these vehicles moving quickly.

Driving Smarter

We can use technology to make public transportation more efficient. In Stockholm, Sweden, buses communicate with traffic lights. If the buses are running late, the lights will change their timing to get the buses back on schedule. In many cities, apps and smart information boards let riders know when the next bus or train will arrive.

73% Percentage of less energy used by electric buses than diesel buses, according to a study in China

48% Percentage of less CO_2 released by electric buses than diesel

Solutions Needed

Public transportation cannot solve all our problems. Some types, such as airplanes, still release a lot of carbon dioxide. And public transportation is only practical in places with a lot of people. People who live in mainly rural areas generally have no access to public transportation.

Going Electric

Many people are switching from gas-powered cars to ones that run on electricity. From the outside, they look just like any other car.

But under the hood, they are very different. They have an electric motor and batteries to provide power, as well as a charger. The electric motor is quiet, so an electric car makes very little noise as it drives.

A hybrid car has an electric motor and a gasoline engine that take turns. The gasoline engine can help charge the batteries.

Better Batteries

Most electric cars use bigger versions of the rechargeable batteries found in laptops and smartphones. Engineers are working on batteries that will allow cars to drive farther before needing to recharge. An innovative new form of battery, called solid-state, is being developed that would be faster to charge and less likely to catch fire.

Over 5 million

Number of electric cars on the road by 2019

2.1% Percentage of new cars sold in 2019 that were electric

Electric Benefits

Electric cars don't give off any gases or particulates, so they are clean to run. Many drivers find charging an electric car is much cheaper than buying gas for a traditional car. In some places, taxes and charges are reduced for electric cars to encourage people to buy them. These cars also have fewer moving parts and need less maintenance.

Plugging In

Electric cars need frequent charging. Charging the batteries from empty to full takes several hours. Many electric car owners install a charger at their home, where they can leave their car plugged in overnight. For long journeys, there are charging points at some service stations. More charging points are being built, but even more are still needed.

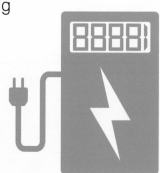

Electric cars need charging more often than a car with a gas engine needs to be refueled. The more places there are to charge electric cars, the likelier it is people will buy them.

WHAT CAN I DO?

Make a Change

If there are more places to charge, more people might switch to electric cars. Write to your local government to ask them to install public charging stations. Can you persuade other people in your community to write letters, too? How will you make your case?

About 57,000 in U.S.A. & 5,800 in Canada Number of public charging stations in 2018

30 minutes Amount of time to recharge a battery by fastest charger

Charging Problems

Charging electric cars is very cheap. There are more places than ever before to charge them, but they are far from perfect. Not all cars use the same technology, so drivers need to find a charging station that matches their car. Also, the electricity they use is often created by burning fossil fuels.

23

Future Developments

To help the environment, we need to reduce emissions. One way is by traveling less, such as taking fewer airplane flights.

But we can also reduce our emissions by traveling smarter. For example, instead of owning their own cars, the members of car clubs share a small number of cars and rent them by the hour. Cities can build bike lanes so more people can safely cycle instead of drive.

Cycling is not just a way to cut carbon dioxide emissions. It is a good way to exercise and keep healthy too!

Shop Local

The things we buy have to travel, too. Food, clothes, and books are shipped across the world to get to our stores. Find out where the things you buy were made or grown. Could you buy things from closer to home? A farmers market is a great place to find locally grown food.

About 2 million Number of people in Germany in car-sharing clubs

More than 20% Percentage of workers in U.S.A. who work from home part of the time

Technology Boost

Thanks to the internet, many office workers can now work from home. They don't have to drive to work every day. They can use video calls to keep in touch. Business people can use videoconferencing rather than fly to international conferences.

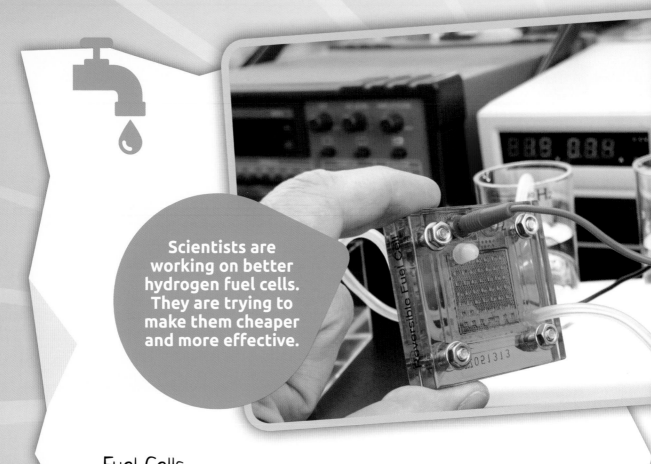

Scientists are working on better hydrogen fuel cells. They are trying to make them cheaper and more effective.

Fuel Cells

One day in the future, we may be able to drive without worrying about emissions or running out of fossil fuels. Scientists are working on a new way to power vehicles. It is called a hydrogen **fuel cell**. This device produces electricity using hydrogen as a fuel. The only waste products are heat and pure water. There are no harmful emissions to pollute the air.

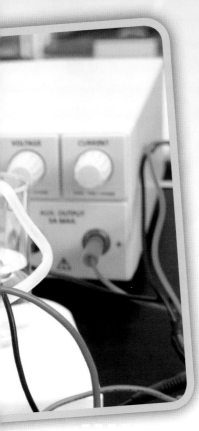

Hydrogen Problems

Unfortunately, fuel cells have problems. Making hydrogen fuel is not easy, and it involves the use of fossil fuels. It is also difficult to store safely. Currently, cars fuled by hydrogen are expensive, and there are few charging stations for them. As more car companies develop the cars, they may become cheaper.

Fewer than 15,000

Number of fuel cell vehicles on the roads around the world

376 **Number of hydrogen fueling stations at the end of 2018**

TECHNOLOGY SOLUTIONS

Hydrogen Frameworks

The more hydrogen a fuel cell vehicle can store, the farther it can drive before it has to refuel. Engineers are working on a new type of hydrogen storage device, called a metal-organic framework (MOF). These high-tech materials have millions of microscopic holes that hold particles of hydrogen.

Your Turn!

How could you change the way the people in your community travel?

Gathering Evidence

Start by taking a survey to find out how people currently travel. You could interview people or make a questionnaire. Here are some questions that you might want to ask:

- How do you get to school?
- How many miles, or kilometers, does your family drive in an average week?
- How do people in your family get to work?
- Is there public transportation you could take?

The more people you interview, the more complete a picture you will get. Make sure to note your own answers too!

People may be more willing to ride a bike to work or school if they have someone to ride with. Don't forget your helmets!

Results

Once you have your answers, analyze the results to get the bigger picture. You might be able to show the results in a graph or chart. What do they tell you about the way that people travel in your community?

Finding Solutions

Now it's time to make a plan. Can you think of changes that might mean people use cars less often? Research the public transportation options available in your area. Are there any ride-sharing programs or car-sharing clubs in your area? Could you set up a group to ride bikes together to school?

Glossary

atmosphere The layers of gases that surround Earth

carbon dioxide A gas found naturally in the atmosphere, which is also produced when living things exhale and fossil fuels are burned

drone A small remote-controlled flying machine

engine A machine with moving parts that uses fuel to produce motion

fossil fuel A fuel such as oil or natural gas, which is formed from the remains of living things that died millions of years ago

fuel A substance that is burned to produce heat or power

fuel cell A cell that uses a chemical reaction to produce electricity

global warming The gradual rise in Earth's temperature due to increased greenhouse gases

habitats The places where particular types of plants and animals live

hybrid A vehicle that has both a gasoline engine and an electric motor

particulates Material in the form of tiny particles

pollution The adding of harmful substances into an environment

public transportation Forms of transportation that carry many passengers, run on a regular schedule, and that anyone can ride

renewable Able to be replaced rather than running out completely

tsunami A large ocean wave caused by an earthquake or other event

Find out More

Books

Dickmann, Nancy. *Burning Out: Energy From Fossil Fuels.* Crabtree, 2016.

Eschbach, Christina. *Inside Electric Cars (Inside Technology).* Core Library, 2019.

Marquardt, Meg. *Hydrogen Fuel Cells (Alternative Energy).* Core Library, 2016.

Wang, Andrea. *How Can We Reduce Fossil Fuel Pollution?* Lerner Classroom, 2016.

Websites

This website explains how hydrogen cars work. auto.howstuffworks.com/fuel-efficiency/hybrid-technology/hydrogen-cars1.htm

Visit this website to find out about climate change and the greenhouse effect. climatekids.nasa.gov/greenhouse-effect/

This site explains how electric cars work and what the future might hold for them. www.explainthatstuff.com/electriccars.html

Index